50 Japanese Bento Box Recipes for Home

By: Kelly Johnson

Table of Contents

- Teriyaki Chicken Bento
- Sushi Roll Bento
- Tamagoyaki Bento
- Beef and Broccoli Bento
- Salmon Onigirazu Bento
- Miso Soup Bento
- Tempura Bento
- Yakitori Bento
- Tofu Katsu Bento
- Shrimp Stir-Fry Bento
- Okonomiyaki Bento
- Karaage Bento
- Udon Noodle Bento
- California Roll Bento
- Spicy Tuna Onigirazu Bento
- Pork Shumai Bento
- Gyoza Bento
- Chicken Katsu Bento
- Vegetable Tempura Bento
- Sesame Noodle Salad Bento
- Eel and Avocado Sushi Bento
- Teriyaki Salmon Bento
- Tonkatsu Bento
- Edamame and Quinoa Salad Bento
- Cucumber and Crab Roll Bento
- Grilled Mackerel Bento
- Shrimp Tempura Roll Bento
- Chicken Yakisoba Bento
- Tuna Salad Onigirazu Bento
- Hijiki Seaweed Salad Bento
- Bulgogi Beef Bento
- Tamago Sushi Bento
- Spinach and Mushroom Salad Bento
- Kani Salad Bento
- Nikujaga Bento

- Chicken Teriyaki Onigirazu Bento
- Shrimp and Vegetable Tempura Bento
- Tofu and Wakame Salad Bento
- Pork and Kimchi Onigirazu Bento
- Avocado and Cucumber Roll Bento
- Beef Negimaki Bento
- Chicken and Vegetable Skewers Bento
- Quinoa and Avocado Salad Bento
- Sesame Chicken Bento
- Chirashi Sushi Bento
- Egg Salad Onigirazu Bento
- Green Bean and Sesame Salad Bento
- Shrimp and Avocado Onigiri Bento
- Teriyaki Tofu and Broccoli Bento
- Soba Noodle Salad Bento

Teriyaki Chicken Bento

Ingredients:

- 1 cup sushi rice, cooked and seasoned with rice vinegar
- 1 cup teriyaki chicken, grilled and sliced
- 1 cup steamed broccoli florets
- 1/2 cup carrot kinpira (julienned and sautéed carrots with soy and sugar)
- 1/4 cup pickled ginger slices
- 2 nori-wrapped onigiri (rice balls)
- Sesame seeds for garnish

Instructions:

Arrange a bed of seasoned sushi rice in one compartment of the bento box.
Place slices of teriyaki chicken on top of the rice, ensuring an even distribution.
Fill another compartment with steamed broccoli florets.
Add the carrot kinpira to a separate section of the bento box.
Include pickled ginger slices in a small compartment for a burst of flavor.
Shape cooked rice into two onigiri, wrap each with a strip of nori, and place in the box.
Sprinkle sesame seeds over the teriyaki chicken for added texture.
Seal the bento box and enjoy a delicious and balanced Teriyaki Chicken Bento!

Sushi Roll Bento

Ingredients:

- 1 cup sushi rice, seasoned with rice vinegar
- 2 sheets nori (seaweed)
- Assorted sushi fillings (e.g., cucumber sticks, avocado slices, crab sticks, sashimi-grade fish)
- Soy sauce for dipping
- Pickled ginger and wasabi for serving
- Sesame seeds for garnish
- Sliced radishes for decoration

Instructions:

Prepare sushi rice and season it with rice vinegar. Let it cool to room temperature.
Lay a bamboo sushi rolling mat on a flat surface and place a sheet of nori on top.
Wet your hands to prevent sticking and spread a thin layer of sushi rice evenly over the nori, leaving a small border at the top.
Arrange your choice of sushi fillings along the bottom edge of the rice.
Carefully lift the edge of the bamboo mat closest to you and roll the nori and rice over the fillings, applying gentle pressure to form a tight sushi roll.
Seal the edge with a little water and repeat the process with the second sheet of nori.
Use a sharp knife to slice each roll into bite-sized pieces.
Arrange the sushi rolls in one compartment of the bento box.
Add soy sauce in a small container for dipping.
Include pickled ginger, wasabi, and sesame seeds in separate compartments for added flavor.
Decorate the bento box with sliced radishes for a colorful touch.
Seal the bento box, and your Sushi Roll Bento is ready to enjoy!

Tamagoyaki Bento

Ingredients:

- 1 cup sushi rice, cooked and seasoned with rice vinegar
- Tamagoyaki (Japanese rolled omelette):
    - 4 large eggs
    - 2 tablespoons sugar
    - 1 tablespoon soy sauce
    - 1 tablespoon mirin (sweet rice wine)
    - Dash of salt
    - Vegetable oil for cooking
- Steamed broccoli florets
- Thinly sliced cucumber
- Edamame beans, steamed
- Soy sauce for drizzling
- Sesame seeds for garnish
- Nori strips for decoration

Instructions:

Cook sushi rice and let it cool to room temperature, then pack it into one compartment of the bento box.
For Tamagoyaki, whisk eggs in a bowl. Add sugar, soy sauce, mirin, and a dash of salt. Mix well.
Heat a rectangular Tamagoyaki pan and lightly oil it. Pour a thin layer of the egg mixture, tilting the pan to spread evenly. Roll it from one end to the other.
Move the rolled omelette to the other end of the pan, oil the empty space, and pour more egg mixture. Roll it again over the existing omelette.
Repeat until all the egg mixture is used, creating layers. Once cooked, let it cool and slice into bite-sized pieces.
Arrange Tamagoyaki slices neatly in another compartment of the bento box.
Add steamed broccoli florets and sliced cucumber in separate compartments.
Place edamame beans in another section.
Drizzle a little soy sauce over the Tamagoyaki for added flavor.
Garnish with sesame seeds and decorate with nori strips.
Seal the bento box, and your Tamagoyaki Bento is ready for a delightful lunch!

Beef and Broccoli Bento

Ingredients:

- 1 cup cooked jasmine rice
- 1 cup beef and broccoli stir-fry:
    - 200g beef sirloin, thinly sliced
    - 1 cup broccoli florets
    - 2 tablespoons soy sauce
    - 1 tablespoon oyster sauce
    - 1 tablespoon hoisin sauce
    - 1 tablespoon sesame oil
    - 1 tablespoon vegetable oil
    - 2 cloves garlic, minced
    - 1 teaspoon ginger, grated
    - Sesame seeds for garnish
- Pickled radishes for a tangy side
- Sliced oranges for a refreshing touch

Instructions:

Cook jasmine rice according to package instructions and let it cool to room temperature. Pack it into one compartment of the bento box.
In a wok or skillet, heat vegetable oil over medium-high heat. Add minced garlic and grated ginger, sauté until fragrant.
Add thinly sliced beef to the wok and stir-fry until browned.
Add broccoli florets to the wok and continue to stir-fry until they are tender-crisp.
In a small bowl, mix soy sauce, oyster sauce, hoisin sauce, and sesame oil. Pour the sauce over the beef and broccoli mixture, stirring to coat evenly. Cook for an additional 2-3 minutes.
Transfer the beef and broccoli stir-fry to another compartment of the bento box. Sprinkle sesame seeds over the beef for added texture and flavor.
Add pickled radishes to a separate section of the bento box for a tangy side dish.
Place slices of oranges in another compartment for a refreshing palate cleanser.
Seal the bento box, and your Beef and Broccoli Bento is ready to enjoy a savory and satisfying meal!

Salmon Onigirazu Bento

Ingredients:

- 1 cup sushi rice, cooked and seasoned with rice vinegar
- Nori sheets
- 150g grilled or smoked salmon, flaked
- 1 avocado, sliced
- 1 cucumber, julienned
- 2 tablespoons sushi seasoning or soy sauce
- Sesame seeds for garnish
- Pickled ginger for serving
- Wasabi for serving
- Mixed greens for a side salad

Instructions:

Lay a sheet of plastic wrap on a flat surface and place a nori sheet on top.
Spread a layer of sushi rice evenly over the nori, leaving a small border.
Arrange flaked salmon, sliced avocado, and julienned cucumber over the rice.
Drizzle sushi seasoning or soy sauce over the fillings.
Fold the sides of the nori sheet towards the center, covering the fillings, and then fold the top and bottom to form a square-shaped parcel.
Wrap the onigirazu tightly in the plastic wrap and let it sit for a minute to set.
Unwrap the onigirazu and cut it into halves or quarters.
Pack the Salmon Onigirazu pieces into one compartment of the bento box.
Sprinkle sesame seeds over the onigirazu for added texture.
Include pickled ginger and a small portion of wasabi in separate compartments for serving.
Add a side salad of mixed greens to another section of the bento box for freshness.
Seal the bento box, and your Salmon Onigirazu Bento is ready to be enjoyed!

Miso Soup Bento

Ingredients:

- 1 cup sushi rice, cooked and seasoned with rice vinegar
- Miso soup:
    - 2 tablespoons miso paste
    - 2 cups dashi (Japanese broth)
    - 1/2 cup tofu, cubed
    - 1/4 cup wakame seaweed, rehydrated
    - 1 green onion, thinly sliced
- Shrimp and vegetable tempura:
    - 6 shrimp, peeled and deveined
    - Assorted vegetables (e.g., sweet potato, zucchini, broccoli)
    - Tempura batter mix
    - Vegetable oil for frying
- Edamame beans, steamed
- Radish slices for garnish
- Pickled plum (umeboshi) for a tangy side

Instructions:

Cook sushi rice according to package instructions and place it in one compartment of the bento box.
In a small pot, combine miso paste and dashi over medium heat. Stir until the miso is dissolved.
Add cubed tofu, rehydrated wakame seaweed, and sliced green onions to the miso broth. Simmer for a few minutes until heated through.
Ladle the miso soup into a thermos or a heat-sealed container to keep it warm until lunchtime.
Prepare shrimp and vegetable tempura by dipping them in tempura batter and frying until golden brown. Drain on paper towels.
Arrange the tempura in a separate compartment of the bento box.
Add steamed edamame beans to another section for a protein-packed side.
Garnish the miso soup with radish slices for a fresh and crunchy element.
Include a pickled plum (umeboshi) in a small compartment for a tangy side.
Seal the bento box, and your Miso Soup Bento is ready to bring a taste of Japan to your lunch break!

Tempura Bento

Ingredients:

- 1 cup sushi rice, cooked and seasoned with rice vinegar
- Shrimp and vegetable tempura:
    - 6 shrimp, peeled and deveined
    - Assorted vegetables (e.g., sweet potato, zucchini, broccoli)
    - Tempura batter mix
    - Vegetable oil for frying
- Tempura dipping sauce:
    - 1/4 cup soy sauce
    - 2 tablespoons mirin (sweet rice wine)
    - 1 teaspoon grated daikon radish
    - 1 teaspoon grated ginger
- Edamame beans, steamed
- Pickled ginger slices for serving
- Sliced cucumber for a refreshing side
- Orange slices for dessert

Instructions:

Cook sushi rice according to package instructions and place it in one compartment of the bento box.

Prepare shrimp and vegetable tempura by dipping them in tempura batter and frying until golden brown. Drain on paper towels.

Arrange the tempura in another compartment of the bento box.

In a small bowl, mix soy sauce, mirin, grated daikon radish, and grated ginger to create the tempura dipping sauce. Pour it into a small, leak-proof container.

Steam edamame beans and place them in a separate compartment for a protein-packed side.

Add pickled ginger slices to another section for a palate-cleansing element.

Include thinly sliced cucumber for a refreshing and crunchy side.

Pack orange slices in a compartment for a naturally sweet dessert.

Seal the bento box, and your Tempura Bento is ready to be enjoyed, complete with the delightful crunch of tempura and a variety of tasty sides!

Yakitori Bento

Ingredients:

- 1 cup sushi rice, cooked and seasoned with rice vinegar
- Yakitori skewers:
    - 6 bamboo skewers
    - 12 pieces of chicken thigh or breast, cut into bite-sized pieces
    - Yakitori sauce (store-bought or homemade):
        - 1/4 cup soy sauce
        - 1/4 cup mirin (sweet rice wine)
        - 2 tablespoons sake (Japanese rice wine)
        - 2 tablespoons sugar
        - 1 clove garlic, minced
        - 1 teaspoon grated ginger
- Grilled vegetables:
    - Assorted vegetables (e.g., bell peppers, mushrooms, onions)
    - Olive oil for grilling
    - Salt and pepper to taste
- Steamed broccoli florets
- Pickled cucumber slices
- Nori sheets for wrapping
- Sesame seeds for garnish

Instructions:

Cook sushi rice according to package instructions and place it in one compartment of the bento box.

Prepare the Yakitori skewers by threading the chicken pieces onto bamboo skewers.

In a small saucepan, combine soy sauce, mirin, sake, sugar, minced garlic, and grated ginger. Bring to a simmer over medium heat and cook for 5 minutes until slightly thickened.

Preheat a grill or grill pan over medium-high heat. Brush the Yakitori skewers with the Yakitori sauce and grill until cooked through, turning occasionally and basting with more sauce.

Grill assorted vegetables brushed with olive oil, seasoned with salt and pepper until tender and slightly charred.

Arrange the Yakitori skewers and grilled vegetables in separate compartments of the bento box.

Steam broccoli florets and place them in another section for a nutritious side.

Add pickled cucumber slices to another compartment for a refreshing and tangy element.

Cut nori sheets into strips for wrapping around the Yakitori skewers if desired.

Sprinkle sesame seeds over the Yakitori skewers and grilled vegetables for added flavor and texture.

Seal the bento box, and your Yakitori Bento is ready to enjoy, featuring delicious grilled chicken skewers, flavorful vegetables, and tasty sides!

Tofu Katsu Bento

Ingredients:

- 1 cup sushi rice, cooked and seasoned with rice vinegar
- Tofu Katsu:
    - 1 block firm tofu, pressed and cut into rectangular pieces
    - 1 cup panko breadcrumbs
    - 1/4 cup all-purpose flour
    - 2 flaxseed eggs (2 tablespoons ground flaxseeds + 6 tablespoons water)
    - Salt and pepper to taste
    - Vegetable oil for frying
- Tonkatsu sauce for dipping (store-bought or homemade):
    - 1/4 cup ketchup
    - 2 tablespoons soy sauce
    - 1 tablespoon Worcestershire sauce
    - 1 tablespoon mirin (optional)
    - 1 tablespoon sugar
- Steamed broccoli florets
- Shredded cabbage for a side salad
- Cherry tomatoes for a refreshing touch
- Orange slices for dessert

Instructions:

Cook sushi rice according to package instructions and place it in one compartment of the bento box.

Press the tofu to remove excess water and cut it into rectangular pieces.

Set up a breading station with three shallow dishes: one with flour, one with flaxseed egg mixture, and one with panko breadcrumbs seasoned with salt and pepper.

Dredge each tofu piece in flour, dip in the flaxseed egg mixture, and coat with panko breadcrumbs.

Heat vegetable oil in a pan and fry the tofu until golden brown and crispy. Drain on paper towels.

In a small bowl, whisk together the Tonkatsu sauce ingredients.

Arrange the Tofu Katsu in one compartment of the bento box.

Place a small container of Tonkatsu sauce for dipping.

Add steamed broccoli florets to another section.
Include shredded cabbage in a compartment for a fresh and crunchy side salad.
Add cherry tomatoes for a burst of color and refreshment.
Pack orange slices in a compartment for a naturally sweet dessert.
Seal the bento box, and your Tofu Katsu Bento is ready to be enjoyed, complete with crispy tofu and a variety of delightful sides!

Shrimp Stir-Fry Bento

Ingredients:

- 1 cup jasmine rice, cooked and cooled
- Shrimp Stir-Fry:
    - 200g shrimp, peeled and deveined
    - 1 cup mixed vegetables (bell peppers, broccoli, snap peas, carrots)
    - 2 tablespoons soy sauce
    - 1 tablespoon oyster sauce
    - 1 tablespoon sesame oil
    - 1 tablespoon vegetable oil
    - 1 teaspoon ginger, minced
    - 2 cloves garlic, minced
    - Green onions, chopped, for garnish
- Sesame seeds for garnish
- Sliced cucumber for a side
- Edamame beans, steamed
- Pickled radishes for a tangy side

Instructions:

Cook jasmine rice according to package instructions and let it cool to room temperature. Place it in one compartment of the bento box.
In a wok or skillet, heat vegetable oil over medium-high heat. Add minced ginger and garlic, sauté until fragrant.
Add shrimp to the wok and stir-fry until they turn pink and opaque.
Add mixed vegetables to the wok and continue to stir-fry until they are tender-crisp.
In a small bowl, mix soy sauce, oyster sauce, and sesame oil. Pour the sauce over the shrimp and vegetables, stirring to coat evenly. Cook for an additional 2-3 minutes.
Transfer the Shrimp Stir-Fry to another compartment of the bento box.
Sprinkle chopped green onions and sesame seeds over the stir-fry for added flavor and presentation.
Arrange sliced cucumber in another compartment for a refreshing side.
Add steamed edamame beans to a separate section for a protein-packed side.
Include pickled radishes in another compartment for a tangy and crunchy element.

Seal the bento box, and your Shrimp Stir-Fry Bento is ready for a delicious and satisfying lunch!

Okonomiyaki Bento

Ingredients:

- 1 cup okonomiyaki batter (prepared according to package instructions)
- 1 cup shredded cabbage
- 1/4 cup sliced green onions
- 1/4 cup tenkasu (tempura scraps) or crispy fried onions
- 1/4 cup cooked and chopped bacon or diced ham (optional)
- Vegetable oil for cooking
- Okonomiyaki sauce (store-bought or homemade):
    - 3 tablespoons ketchup
    - 2 tablespoons Worcestershire sauce
    - 1 tablespoon soy sauce
- Japanese mayo for drizzling
- Aonori (dried seaweed flakes) for garnish
- Pickled ginger for serving
- Steamed rice on the side

Instructions:

In a large bowl, combine the okonomiyaki batter, shredded cabbage, sliced green onions, tenkasu or crispy fried onions, and bacon or ham if using.
Heat a non-stick skillet or griddle over medium heat and add a little vegetable oil.
Pour a portion of the okonomiyaki batter onto the skillet to form a round pancake. Cook until the edges are golden brown, then flip and cook the other side until fully cooked.
Repeat the process to make additional okonomiyaki pancakes. Once cooked, let them cool, then slice into wedges.
Mix the ingredients for the okonomiyaki sauce in a small bowl.
Arrange the okonomiyaki wedges in one compartment of the bento box.
Drizzle okonomiyaki sauce and Japanese mayo over the wedges.
Sprinkle aonori over the top for added flavor and visual appeal.
Include pickled ginger in a separate compartment for serving.
Add a side of steamed rice in a separate compartment or on the side.
Seal the bento box, and your Okonomiyaki Bento is ready for a tasty and satisfying meal!

Karaage Bento

Ingredients:

- 1 cup sushi rice, cooked and seasoned with rice vinegar
- Chicken Karaage:
    - 250g boneless, skinless chicken thighs, cut into bite-sized pieces
    - 3 tablespoons soy sauce
    - 1 tablespoon sake (Japanese rice wine)
    - 1 tablespoon ginger, grated
    - 2 cloves garlic, minced
    - 1 tablespoon sesame oil
    - 1 cup potato starch or cornstarch, for coating
    - Vegetable oil for frying
- Shredded lettuce for the base
- Sliced radishes for freshness
- Cherry tomatoes for a burst of color
- Lemon wedges for garnish
- Japanese mayo for dipping
- Soy sauce for drizzling over rice

Instructions:

Cook sushi rice according to package instructions and let it cool to room temperature. Place it in one compartment of the bento box.
In a bowl, marinate the chicken pieces in soy sauce, sake, grated ginger, minced garlic, and sesame oil for at least 30 minutes.
Heat vegetable oil in a deep fryer or skillet to 350°F (180°C).
Coat the marinated chicken pieces in potato starch or cornstarch.
Fry the chicken until golden brown and fully cooked. Drain on paper towels.
Place a bed of shredded lettuce in another compartment of the bento box.
Arrange the crispy Chicken Karaage on top of the lettuce.
Slice radishes and place them in a separate compartment for freshness.
Add cherry tomatoes for a burst of color.
Include lemon wedges for garnish and a hint of citrus.
Pack a small container of Japanese mayo for dipping the karaage.
Drizzle soy sauce over the sushi rice for added flavor.
Seal the bento box, and your Karaage Bento is ready for a delightful and flavorful lunch!

Udon Noodle Bento

Ingredients:

- 1 cup cooked udon noodles, cooled
- Teriyaki Chicken:
    - 1 boneless, skinless chicken breast, thinly sliced
    - 2 tablespoons soy sauce
    - 1 tablespoon mirin (sweet rice wine)
    - 1 tablespoon sake (Japanese rice wine)
    - 1 tablespoon sugar
    - 1 tablespoon vegetable oil for cooking
- Stir-fried Vegetables:
    - 1 cup broccoli florets
    - 1 carrot, julienned
    - 1 bell pepper, thinly sliced
    - 2 tablespoons soy sauce
    - 1 tablespoon sesame oil
- Sesame seeds for garnish
- Sliced green onions for garnish
- Nori strips for a touch of umami
- Pickled ginger for serving
- Soy sauce for drizzling over udon noodles

Instructions:

Cook udon noodles according to package instructions, then rinse them under cold water and set aside.
Marinate chicken slices in soy sauce, mirin, sake, and sugar for at least 15 minutes.
Heat vegetable oil in a skillet over medium-high heat. Cook the marinated chicken until fully cooked and slightly caramelized. Set aside.
In the same skillet, stir-fry broccoli, carrot, and bell pepper in soy sauce and sesame oil until vegetables are tender-crisp. Set aside.
Pack the cooled udon noodles into one compartment of the bento box.
Arrange the teriyaki chicken slices on top of the udon noodles.
Place the stir-fried vegetables in another compartment.

Sprinkle sesame seeds and sliced green onions over the udon and chicken for added flavor and texture.
Add nori strips to enhance the umami flavor.
Include pickled ginger in a separate compartment for serving.
Drizzle soy sauce over the udon noodles just before eating for extra seasoning.
Seal the bento box, and your Udon Noodle Bento is ready for a delicious and satisfying lunch with a mix of textures and flavors!

California Roll Bento

Ingredients:

California Rolls:
- Nori (seaweed) sheets
- Sushi rice
- Imitation crab or real crab, shredded
- Avocado, sliced
- Cucumber, julienned
- Sushi vinegar, sugar, and salt (for seasoning rice)

Side Dishes:
- Edamame beans (steamed and lightly salted)
- Pickled ginger
- Wasabi
- Soy sauce for dipping

Garnish:
- Sesame seeds
- Chopped green onions

Vegetable and Fruit Sides:
- Cherry tomatoes
- Sliced carrots or bell peppers
- Sliced pineapple or melon

Snack Section:
- Seaweed snacks
- Miso soup in a thermos

Instructions:

Prepare Sushi Rice:
- Cook sushi rice according to package instructions.
- While it's still warm, season with a mixture of sushi vinegar, sugar, and salt. Allow it to cool to room temperature.

Make California Rolls:
- Place a sheet of nori on a bamboo sushi mat.
- Wet your hands and spread a thin layer of sushi rice over the nori, leaving a small border at the top.

- Arrange shredded crab, avocado slices, and julienned cucumber along the center of the rice.
- Roll the sushi tightly using the bamboo mat, sealing the edge with a bit of water.
- Slice the roll into bite-sized pieces.

Arrange in the Bento Box:
- Place the California rolls neatly in one section of the bento box.

Prepare Side Dishes:
- Steam edamame and lightly salt them.
- Add pickled ginger, wasabi, and soy sauce in separate small containers.

Garnish:
- Sprinkle sesame seeds and chopped green onions over the California rolls.

Vegetable and Fruit Sides:
- Arrange cherry tomatoes, sliced carrots, and pineapple or melon slices in different sections of the bento box.

Snack Section:
- Include seaweed snacks in a compartment.
- Pack miso soup in a thermos for a warm, comforting addition.

Presentation:
- Arrange everything in the bento box with attention to colors and textures, creating an aesthetically pleasing and balanced meal.

Storage and Transport:
- Use dividers or small containers within the bento box to keep flavors separate.
- Wrap delicate items like sushi rolls in plastic wrap to prevent them from sticking or drying out.

Enjoy your delicious and visually appealing California Roll Bento! It's a versatile lunch option that you can customize based on your preferences.

Spicy Tuna Onigirazu Bento

Ingredients:

For Spicy Tuna Filling:

- Canned tuna (in water or oil)
- Mayonnaise
- Sriracha sauce or chili paste (adjust to taste)
- Soy sauce
- Sesame oil
- Green onions, finely chopped
- Salt and pepper to taste

For Onigirazu:

- Nori (seaweed) sheets
- Sushi rice
- Rice vinegar, sugar, and salt (for seasoning rice)
- Avocado, sliced
- Lettuce leaves
- Pickled ginger

Side Dishes:

- Sliced cucumber or radishes
- Cherry tomatoes
- Soy sauce for dipping

Garnish:

- Sesame seeds
- Chopped cilantro or parsley

Instructions:

1. Prepare Spicy Tuna Filling:

- In a bowl, mix canned tuna, mayonnaise, sriracha sauce, soy sauce, sesame oil, chopped green onions, salt, and pepper. Adjust the spice level to your liking.

2. Make Sushi Rice:

   - Cook sushi rice according to package instructions.
   - While it's still warm, season the rice with a mixture of rice vinegar, sugar, and salt. Allow it to cool to room temperature.

3. Assemble Onigirazu:

   - Place a sheet of nori on a clean surface.
   - Spread a layer of sushi rice over the nori, leaving a border around the edges.
   - Add a spoonful of spicy tuna in the center of the rice.
   - Place avocado slices, lettuce leaves, and pickled ginger on top of the tuna.
   - Cover with another layer of sushi rice.
   - Fold the corners of the nori sheet over the rice, forming a square or rectangular shape.

4. Slice Onigirazu:

   - Carefully cut the onigirazu in half with a sharp knife.

5. Arrange in the Bento Box:

   - Place the Spicy Tuna Onigirazu halves in one section of the bento box.

6. Prepare Side Dishes:

   - Arrange sliced cucumber or radishes and cherry tomatoes in separate sections of the bento box.

7. Garnish:

   - Sprinkle sesame seeds and chopped cilantro or parsley over the onigirazu for added flavor and visual appeal.

8. Soy Sauce:

   - Add a small container of soy sauce for dipping.

9. Presentation:

   - Arrange everything in the bento box, ensuring a balance of colors and textures.

10. Storage and Transport:

- Use dividers or small containers within the bento box to prevent flavors from mixing.
- Wrap the onigirazu halves in plastic wrap to keep them secure.

Enjoy your Spicy Tuna Onigirazu Bento, a delightful and flavorful lunch option that's perfect for on-the-go or as a satisfying meal at home!

Pork Shumai Bento

Ingredients:

For Pork Shumai:

    Ground pork
    Shrimp, finely chopped (optional)
    Water chestnuts, finely chopped
    Ginger, minced
    Garlic, minced
    Soy sauce
    Sesame oil
    Cornstarch
    Wonton or gyoza wrappers

For Dipping Sauce:

    Soy sauce
    Rice vinegar
    Sesame oil
    Sriracha (optional)

For Bento:

    Sushi rice
    Steamed broccoli or edamame
    Sliced radishes or cucumber
    Pickled ginger
    Cherry tomatoes

Garnish:

    Chopped green onions
    Sesame seeds

Instructions:

1. Prepare Pork Shumai:

    - In a bowl, combine ground pork, chopped shrimp, water chestnuts, minced ginger, minced garlic, soy sauce, sesame oil, and cornstarch.
    - Place a spoonful of the pork mixture onto a wonton or gyoza wrapper.
    - Fold the wrapper over the filling, pleating the edges to create a basket shape.

2. Steam Pork Shumai:

    - Steam the pork shumai in a bamboo steamer or a steamer basket for about 12-15 minutes or until cooked through.

3. Make Dipping Sauce:

    - Mix soy sauce, rice vinegar, sesame oil, and sriracha (if using) to create a dipping sauce. Adjust the proportions to suit your taste.

4. Cook Sushi Rice:

    - Cook sushi rice according to package instructions.

5. Assemble Bento:

    - Place a portion of sushi rice in one section of the bento box.

6. Arrange Pork Shumai:

    - Arrange the steamed pork shumai in another section.

7. Add Side Dishes:

    - Arrange steamed broccoli or edamame, sliced radishes or cucumber, pickled ginger, and cherry tomatoes in different sections of the bento box.

8. Garnish:

- Sprinkle chopped green onions and sesame seeds over the pork shumai and rice.

9. Presentation:

- Arrange everything in the bento box, considering colors and textures for an appealing presentation.

10. Storage and Transport:

- Use dividers or small containers within the bento box to keep flavors separate.
- Wrap the bento securely to prevent spills during transport.

Enjoy your Pork Shumai Bento, a delightful combination of flavors and textures that makes for a satisfying lunch!

Gyoza Bento

Ingredients:

For Gyoza:

    Gyoza wrappers
    Ground pork or chicken
    Napa cabbage, finely chopped
    Garlic, minced
    Ginger, minced
    Soy sauce
    Sesame oil
    Green onions, finely chopped
    Salt and pepper
    Cooking oil for pan-frying

For Dipping Sauce:

    Soy sauce
    Rice vinegar
    Sesame oil
    Optional: chili oil or chili flakes for extra spice

For Bento:

    Sushi rice
    Steamed or stir-fried vegetables (e.g., broccoli, carrots, snow peas)
    Sliced cucumber or radishes
    Pickled ginger
    Cherry tomatoes

Garnish:

    Chopped green onions
    Sesame seeds

Instructions:

1. Prepare Gyoza Filling:

   - In a bowl, combine ground pork or chicken, finely chopped Napa cabbage, minced garlic, minced ginger, soy sauce, sesame oil, chopped green onions, salt, and pepper.

2. Assemble Gyoza:

   - Place a spoonful of the filling in the center of a gyoza wrapper.
   - Moisten the edges of the wrapper with water.
   - Fold the wrapper in half, pleating the edges to create a crescent shape.

3. Pan-Fry Gyoza:

   - Heat cooking oil in a pan over medium heat.
   - Place the gyoza in the pan, flat side down, and cook until the bottoms are golden brown.
   - Add water to the pan and cover to steam until the filling is cooked through.

4. Make Dipping Sauce:

   - Mix soy sauce, rice vinegar, sesame oil, and optional chili oil or chili flakes to create a dipping sauce.

5. Cook Sushi Rice:

   - Cook sushi rice according to package instructions.

6. Assemble Bento:

   - Place a portion of sushi rice in one section of the bento box.

7. Arrange Gyoza:

- Arrange the pan-fried gyoza in another section.

8. Add Side Dishes:

- Add steamed or stir-fried vegetables, sliced cucumber or radishes, pickled ginger, and cherry tomatoes to different sections of the bento box.

9. Garnish:

- Sprinkle chopped green onions and sesame seeds over the gyoza and rice.

10. Presentation:

- Arrange everything in the bento box, considering colors and textures for an appealing presentation.

11. Storage and Transport:

- Use dividers or small containers within the bento box to keep flavors separate.
- Wrap the bento securely to prevent spills during transport.

Enjoy your Gyoza Bento, a delightful and flavorful lunch option that brings together the delicious taste of gyoza with complementary sides!

Chicken Katsu Bento

Ingredients:

For Chicken Katsu:

    Chicken breasts or thighs, boneless and skinless
    Salt and pepper
    All-purpose flour
    Eggs, beaten
    Panko breadcrumbs
    Cooking oil for frying

For Tonkatsu Sauce:

    Ketchup
    Worcestershire sauce
    Soy sauce
    Sugar

For Bento:

    Sushi rice
    Shredded cabbage (optional, for serving with Chicken Katsu)
    Steamed broccoli or green beans
    Pickled radishes or cucumbers
    Cherry tomatoes

Garnish:

    Sesame seeds
    Chopped green onions

Instructions:

1. Prepare Chicken Katsu:

- Season the chicken breasts or thighs with salt and pepper.
- Dredge each piece of chicken in flour, dip in beaten eggs, and coat with Panko breadcrumbs.

- Heat cooking oil in a pan over medium heat. Fry the breaded chicken until golden brown and cooked through. Place on a paper towel to drain excess oil.

2. Make Tonkatsu Sauce:

- In a small bowl, mix ketchup, Worcestershire sauce, soy sauce, and sugar to taste. Adjust the proportions according to your preference.

3. Cook Sushi Rice:

- Cook sushi rice according to package instructions.

4. Assemble Bento:

- Place a portion of sushi rice in one section of the bento box.

5. Add Chicken Katsu:

- Slice the Chicken Katsu into strips or bite-sized pieces and arrange them in another section.

6. Include Side Dishes:

- Add shredded cabbage (optional), steamed broccoli or green beans, pickled radishes or cucumbers, and cherry tomatoes in different sections of the bento box.

7. Drizzle with Tonkatsu Sauce:

- Drizzle a bit of Tonkatsu sauce over the Chicken Katsu, or you can pack the sauce in a small container for dipping.

8. Garnish:

- Sprinkle sesame seeds and chopped green onions over the Chicken Katsu and rice.

9. Presentation:

- Arrange everything in the bento box, creating an attractive and well-balanced presentation.

10. Storage and Transport:

- Use dividers or small containers within the bento box to keep flavors separate.
- Wrap the bento securely to prevent spills during transport.

Enjoy your Chicken Katsu Bento, a satisfying and flavorful lunch option that combines the crispy goodness of Chicken Katsu with a variety of delicious sides!

Vegetable Tempura Bento

Ingredients:

For Vegetable Tempura:

- Assorted vegetables (e.g., sweet potatoes, zucchini, bell peppers, broccoli, carrots)
- Tempura batter mix (store-bought or homemade)
- Ice-cold water for the tempura batter
- Vegetable oil for frying

For Dipping Sauce:

- Soy sauce
- Mirin (sweet rice wine)
- Dashi (Japanese fish stock) or water
- Grated daikon radish (optional)

For Bento:

- Sushi rice
- Shredded lettuce or cabbage
- Sliced cucumber or radishes
- Cherry tomatoes
- Pickled ginger

Garnish:

- Sesame seeds
- Chopped green onions

Instructions:

1. Prepare Vegetable Tempura:

- Cut the vegetables into bite-sized pieces or thin slices.
- Mix the tempura batter according to the package instructions or your preferred homemade recipe. The batter should be light and slightly lumpy.
- Heat vegetable oil in a deep pan or fryer to around 350-375°F (175-190°C).
- Dip the vegetables in the tempura batter, letting excess batter drip off, and then fry until golden brown. Place on a paper towel to absorb excess oil.

2. Make Dipping Sauce:

- In a bowl, mix soy sauce, mirin, and dashi (or water) to create a dipping sauce. Adjust the proportions to your taste. Add grated daikon radish if desired.

3. Cook Sushi Rice:

- Cook sushi rice according to package instructions.

4. Assemble Bento:

- Place a portion of sushi rice in one section of the bento box.

5. Arrange Vegetable Tempura:

- Arrange the vegetable tempura in another section.

6. Include Side Dishes:

- Add shredded lettuce or cabbage, sliced cucumber or radishes, cherry tomatoes, and pickled ginger in different sections of the bento box.

7. Drizzle with Dipping Sauce:

- Drizzle a bit of the dipping sauce over the vegetable tempura. You can also pack the sauce in a small container for dipping.

8. Garnish:

- Sprinkle sesame seeds and chopped green onions over the vegetable tempura and rice.

9. Presentation:

- Arrange everything in the bento box, creating an appealing and well-balanced presentation.

10. Storage and Transport:

- Use dividers or small containers within the bento box to keep flavors separate.
- Wrap the bento securely to prevent spills during transport.

Enjoy your Vegetable Tempura Bento, a delicious and crunchy lunch option with a variety of flavors and textures!

Sesame Noodle Salad Bento

Ingredients:

For Sesame Noodle Salad:

    Soba noodles or other thin noodles
    Carrots, julienned
    Cucumber, thinly sliced
    Red bell pepper, thinly sliced
    Edamame beans (steamed and shelled)
    Sesame seeds (toasted)
    Fresh cilantro or parsley, chopped (optional)

For Sesame Dressing:

    Soy sauce
    Sesame oil
    Rice vinegar
    Honey or sugar
    Garlic, minced
    Ginger, grated
    Sriracha or chili paste (optional, for heat)

For Bento:

    Sliced tofu or grilled chicken (optional protein)
    Cherry tomatoes
    Pickled ginger
    Sliced radishes

Garnish:

    Sesame seeds
    Chopped green onions

Instructions:

1. Cook Noodles:

   - Cook the soba noodles or thin noodles according to package instructions. Rinse them under cold water to stop cooking and cool them down.

2. Prepare Sesame Dressing:

   - In a bowl, whisk together soy sauce, sesame oil, rice vinegar, honey or sugar, minced garlic, grated ginger, and sriracha (if using). Adjust the flavors to your preference.

3. Toss Sesame Noodle Salad:

   - In a large bowl, toss the cooled noodles with julienned carrots, thinly sliced cucumber, red bell pepper, edamame beans, and toasted sesame seeds.
   - Pour the sesame dressing over the salad and toss until well combined.

4. Assemble Bento:

   - Place a portion of the sesame noodle salad in one section of the bento box.

5. Add Protein (Optional):

   - Include sliced tofu or grilled chicken in another section of the bento box.

6. Include Side Dishes:

   - Add cherry tomatoes, pickled ginger, and sliced radishes in different sections of the bento box.

7. Garnish:

   - Sprinkle additional sesame seeds and chopped green onions over the sesame noodle salad and protein.

8. Presentation:

- Arrange everything in the bento box, creating an attractive and well-balanced presentation.

9. Storage and Transport:

- Use dividers or small containers within the bento box to keep flavors separate.
- Wrap the bento securely to prevent spills during transport.

Enjoy your Sesame Noodle Salad Bento, a light and flavorful lunch option with a satisfying blend of textures and flavors!

Eel and Avocado Sushi Bento

Ingredients:

For Eel and Avocado Sushi:

- Unagi (grilled eel) - pre-cooked or pre-packaged
- Sushi rice
- Nori (seaweed) sheets
- Avocado, sliced
- Soy sauce
- Wasabi
- Pickled ginger

For Bento:

- Steamed broccoli or edamame
- Sliced cucumber or radishes
- Cherry tomatoes
- Additional soy sauce for dipping

Garnish:

- Sesame seeds
- Chopped green onions

Instructions:

1. Prepare Sushi Rice:

- Cook sushi rice according to package instructions.
- Let it cool to room temperature.

2. Assemble Eel and Avocado Sushi:

- Place a nori sheet on a bamboo sushi mat.

- Wet your hands and spread a thin layer of sushi rice over the nori, leaving a small border at the top.
- Place a slice of avocado and a strip of grilled eel in the center.
- Roll the sushi tightly using the bamboo mat, sealing the edge with a bit of water.
- Slice the roll into bite-sized pieces.

3. Arrange in the Bento Box:

- Place the Eel and Avocado Sushi neatly in one section of the bento box.

4. Prepare Side Dishes:

- Steam broccoli or edamame and arrange them in a section of the bento box.
- Slice cucumber or radishes and place them in another section.
- Add cherry tomatoes to a separate section.

5. Add Condiments:

- Include a small container of soy sauce for dipping and a bit of wasabi.
- Add pickled ginger to a corner of the bento box.

6. Garnish:

- Sprinkle sesame seeds and chopped green onions over the Eel and Avocado Sushi.

7. Presentation:

- Arrange everything in the bento box, considering colors and textures for an appealing presentation.

8. Storage and Transport:

- Use dividers or small containers within the bento box to keep flavors separate.
- Wrap delicate items like sushi rolls in plastic wrap to prevent them from sticking or drying out.

Enjoy your Eel and Avocado Sushi Bento, a tasty and elegant lunch option that combines the richness of eel with the creaminess of avocado!

Teriyaki Salmon Bento

Ingredients:

For Teriyaki Salmon:

    Salmon fillets
    Soy sauce
    Mirin (sweet rice wine)
    Sake (Japanese rice wine) or white wine
    Sugar
    Garlic, minced
    Ginger, grated

For Bento:

    Sushi rice
    Steamed broccoli or green beans
    Sliced cucumber or radishes
    Pickled ginger
    Cherry tomatoes

Garnish:

    Sesame seeds
    Chopped green onions

Instructions:

1. Prepare Teriyaki Salmon:

- In a bowl, mix soy sauce, mirin, sake or white wine, sugar, minced garlic, and grated ginger to create the teriyaki sauce.
- Marinate the salmon fillets in the teriyaki sauce for at least 30 minutes.
- Heat a pan over medium heat and cook the salmon until it's cooked through and has a caramelized glaze.

2. Cook Sushi Rice:

- Cook sushi rice according to package instructions.

3. Assemble Bento:

- Place a portion of sushi rice in one section of the bento box.

4. Add Teriyaki Salmon:

- Place the teriyaki salmon fillets on top of the sushi rice.

5. Include Side Dishes:

- Add steamed broccoli or green beans, sliced cucumber or radishes, cherry tomatoes, and pickled ginger in different sections of the bento box.

6. Garnish:

- Sprinkle sesame seeds and chopped green onions over the teriyaki salmon and rice.

7. Presentation:

- Arrange everything in the bento box, creating an appealing and well-balanced presentation.

8. Storage and Transport:

- Use dividers or small containers within the bento box to keep flavors separate.
- Wrap the bento securely to prevent spills during transport.

Enjoy your Teriyaki Salmon Bento, a delicious and nutritious lunch option that showcases the wonderful flavors of teriyaki-glazed salmon!

Tonkatsu Bento

Ingredients:

For Tonkatsu:

    Pork loin or pork tenderloin, boneless
    Salt and pepper
    Flour for coating
    Eggs, beaten
    Panko breadcrumbs
    Vegetable oil for deep frying

For Tonkatsu Sauce:

    Worcestershire sauce
    Ketchup
    Soy sauce
    Sugar

For Bento:

    Sushi rice
    Shredded cabbage
    Steamed broccoli or edamame
    Pickled radishes or cucumbers
    Cherry tomatoes

Garnish:

    Sesame seeds
    Chopped green onions

Instructions:

1. Prepare Tonkatsu:

- Season the pork loin or tenderloin with salt and pepper.
- Dredge the pork in flour, dip it in beaten eggs, and coat it with Panko breadcrumbs.
- Heat vegetable oil in a deep pan to around 350-375°F (175-190°C).
- Fry the breaded pork until golden brown and cooked through. Place it on a paper towel to absorb excess oil.

2. Make Tonkatsu Sauce:

- In a bowl, mix Worcestershire sauce, ketchup, soy sauce, and sugar to taste. Adjust the proportions to suit your taste preferences.

3. Cook Sushi Rice:

- Cook sushi rice according to package instructions.

4. Assemble Bento:

- Place a portion of sushi rice in one section of the bento box.

5. Arrange Tonkatsu:

- Slice the Tonkatsu into strips and arrange them in another section.

6. Add Side Dishes:

- Include shredded cabbage, steamed broccoli or edamame, pickled radishes or cucumbers, and cherry tomatoes in different sections of the bento box.

7. Drizzle with Tonkatsu Sauce:

- Drizzle a bit of Tonkatsu sauce over the sliced Tonkatsu. You can also pack extra sauce in a small container for dipping.

8. Garnish:

- Sprinkle sesame seeds and chopped green onions over the Tonkatsu and rice.

9. Presentation:

- Arrange everything in the bento box, creating an attractive and well-balanced presentation.

10. Storage and Transport:

- Use dividers or small containers within the bento box to keep flavors separate.
- Wrap the bento securely to prevent spills during transport.

Enjoy your Tonkatsu Bento, a satisfying and flavorful lunch option that combines crispy pork cutlets with a variety of tasty sides!

Edamame and Quinoa Salad Bento

Ingredients:

For Edamame and Quinoa Salad:

- Quinoa, rinsed
- Edamame beans (frozen or fresh), cooked and shelled
- Cherry tomatoes, halved
- Cucumber, diced
- Red bell pepper, diced
- Avocado, diced
- Feta cheese, crumbled (optional)
- Fresh cilantro or parsley, chopped

For Dressing:

- Olive oil
- Lemon juice
- Dijon mustard
- Honey or maple syrup
- Salt and pepper to taste

For Bento:

- Sushi rice or mixed grains (optional)
- Grilled chicken, tofu, or your choice of protein
- Sliced radishes
- Pickled ginger

Garnish:

- Sesame seeds
- Chopped green onions

Instructions:

1. Cook Quinoa:

- Rinse quinoa under cold water. Cook quinoa according to package instructions.

- Let it cool to room temperature.

2. Prepare Edamame and Quinoa Salad:

    - In a large bowl, combine cooked quinoa, shelled edamame beans, cherry tomatoes, diced cucumber, diced red bell pepper, diced avocado, crumbled feta cheese (if using), and chopped cilantro or parsley.

3. Make Dressing:

    - In a small bowl, whisk together olive oil, lemon juice, Dijon mustard, honey or maple syrup, salt, and pepper to create the dressing.

4. Toss Salad with Dressing:

    - Pour the dressing over the salad and toss gently until well coated.

5. Assemble Bento:

    - Place a portion of the edamame and quinoa salad in one section of the bento box.

6. Add Protein:

    - Include grilled chicken, tofu, or your choice of protein in another section of the bento box.

7. Include Side Dishes:

    - Add sushi rice or mixed grains, sliced radishes, and pickled ginger in different sections of the bento box.

8. Garnish:

    - Sprinkle sesame seeds and chopped green onions over the edamame and quinoa salad.

9. Presentation:

- Arrange everything in the bento box, creating an appealing and well-balanced presentation.

10. Storage and Transport:

- Use dividers or small containers within the bento box to keep flavors separate.
- Wrap the bento securely to prevent spills during transport.

Enjoy your Edamame and Quinoa Salad Bento, a nutritious and flavorful lunch option that's perfect for a light and satisfying meal!

Cucumber and Crab Roll Bento

Ingredients:

For Cucumber and Crab Rolls:

> Sushi rice
> Nori (seaweed) sheets
> Imitation crab sticks, shredded
> Cucumber, julienned
> Avocado, sliced
> Rice vinegar, sugar, and salt (for seasoning rice)
> Soy sauce and wasabi for dipping

For Bento:

> Sliced radishes
> Pickled ginger
> Cherry tomatoes
> Edamame beans (steamed and lightly salted)

Garnish:

> Sesame seeds
> Chopped green onions

Instructions:

1. Prepare Sushi Rice:

   - Cook sushi rice according to package instructions.
   - While it's still warm, season with a mixture of rice vinegar, sugar, and salt. Allow it to cool to room temperature.

2. Assemble Cucumber and Crab Rolls:

- Place a sheet of nori on a bamboo sushi mat.
- Wet your hands and spread a thin layer of sushi rice over the nori, leaving a small border at the top.
- Arrange shredded crab, julienned cucumber, and avocado slices along the center of the rice.
- Roll the sushi tightly using the bamboo mat, sealing the edge with a bit of water.
- Slice the roll into bite-sized pieces.

3. Arrange in the Bento Box:

- Place the Cucumber and Crab Rolls neatly in one section of the bento box.

4. Prepare Side Dishes:

- Arrange sliced radishes, pickled ginger, cherry tomatoes, and steamed edamame beans in separate sections of the bento box.

5. Garnish:

- Sprinkle sesame seeds and chopped green onions over the Cucumber and Crab Rolls.

6. Include Soy Sauce and Wasabi:

- Add a small container of soy sauce and a bit of wasabi for dipping.

7. Presentation:

- Arrange everything in the bento box, considering colors and textures for an appealing presentation.

8. Storage and Transport:

- Use dividers or small containers within the bento box to keep flavors separate.
- Wrap delicate items like sushi rolls in plastic wrap to prevent them from sticking or drying out.

Enjoy your Cucumber and Crab Roll Bento, a light and delicious lunch option that captures the flavors of sushi in a convenient box!

Grilled Mackerel Bento

Ingredients:

For Grilled Mackerel:

    Mackerel fillets
    Soy sauce
    Mirin (sweet rice wine)
    Sake (Japanese rice wine) or white wine
    Ginger, grated
    Garlic, minced
    Salt and pepper
    Lemon wedges for serving

For Bento:

    Sushi rice or mixed grains
    Steamed vegetables (e.g., broccoli, carrots, green beans)
    Pickled radishes or cucumbers
    Cherry tomatoes

Garnish:

    Sesame seeds
    Chopped green onions

Instructions:

1. Prepare Grilled Mackerel:

- In a bowl, mix soy sauce, mirin, sake or white wine, grated ginger, minced garlic, salt, and pepper to create a marinade.
- Marinate the mackerel fillets in this mixture for at least 30 minutes.
- Grill the mackerel fillets on a hot grill or pan until cooked through, with a nice char on the outside.

2. Cook Sushi Rice or Mixed Grains:

- Cook sushi rice or mixed grains according to package instructions.

3. Assemble Bento:

- Place a portion of sushi rice or mixed grains in one section of the bento box.

4. Add Grilled Mackerel:

- Place the grilled mackerel fillets on top of the rice.

5. Include Steamed Vegetables:

- Add steamed vegetables (broccoli, carrots, green beans, etc.) in another section of the bento box.

6. Add Side Dishes:

- Include pickled radishes or cucumbers and cherry tomatoes in different sections of the bento box.

7. Garnish:

- Sprinkle sesame seeds and chopped green onions over the grilled mackerel and rice.

8. Serve with Lemon Wedges:

- Include lemon wedges in the bento box for squeezing over the grilled mackerel before eating.

9. Presentation:

- Arrange everything in the bento box, creating an appealing and well-balanced presentation.

10. Storage and Transport:

- Use dividers or small containers within the bento box to keep flavors separate.
- Wrap the bento securely to prevent spills during transport.

Enjoy your Grilled Mackerel Bento, a flavorful and satisfying lunch option that showcases the rich taste of grilled mackerel alongside a variety of complementary sides!

Shrimp Tempura Roll Bento

Ingredients:

For Shrimp Tempura Rolls:

- 1 cup sushi rice
- Nori (seaweed) sheets
- Shrimp tempura (you can buy pre-made or make your own by coating shrimp in tempura batter and frying until golden)
- Avocado, sliced
- Cucumber, julienned
- Sesame seeds
- Soy sauce for dipping

For Bento Box:

- Sushi rice (seasoned with rice vinegar, sugar, and salt)
- Pickled ginger
- Wasabi
- Soy sauce for dipping
- Edamame (steamed and lightly salted)
- Sliced radishes and carrot for a colorful garnish
- Fresh fruit (such as sliced oranges or berries)

Instructions:

Shrimp Tempura Rolls:

> Cook sushi rice according to package instructions and season it with a mixture of rice vinegar, sugar, and salt while it's still warm.
> Place a sheet of nori on a bamboo sushi rolling mat.
> Wet your hands to prevent the rice from sticking and spread a thin layer of sushi rice evenly over the nori, leaving a small border at the top.
> Arrange slices of avocado, cucumber, and shrimp tempura across the center of the rice.
> Sprinkle sesame seeds over the fillings.
> Carefully lift the edge of the bamboo mat closest to you and start rolling the nori over the fillings, using the mat to shape the roll.
> Seal the edge with a little water.
> Using a sharp knife, slice the roll into bite-sized pieces.

Bento Box Assembly:

- Place a portion of seasoned sushi rice in one section of the bento box.
- Arrange the shrimp tempura rolls neatly in another section.
- Add pickled ginger and wasabi in small compartments.
- Place a handful of edamame in another section.
- Garnish with sliced radishes and carrot for color.
- Add a small dipping sauce container for soy sauce.
- Include fresh fruit slices in another compartment for a refreshing touch.

Serving:

Enjoy your Shrimp Tempura Roll Bento by dipping the rolls in soy sauce and savoring the various flavors and textures. It's a well-balanced and visually appealing meal that captures the essence of Japanese cuisine.

Chicken Yakisoba Bento

Ingredients:

For Chicken Yakisoba:

- 200g soba noodles or yakisoba noodles (cooked according to package instructions)
- 1 boneless, skinless chicken breast, thinly sliced
- 1 cup shredded cabbage
- 1 carrot, julienned
- 1 bell pepper, thinly sliced
- 1 small onion, thinly sliced
- 2 cloves garlic, minced
- 2 tablespoons vegetable oil
- 3 tablespoons soy sauce
- 2 tablespoons oyster sauce
- 1 tablespoon Worcestershire sauce
- 1 tablespoon ketchup
- 1 teaspoon sugar
- Salt and pepper to taste
- Green onions, chopped (for garnish)

For Bento Box:

- Cooked rice (white or brown)
- Pickled ginger
- Sesame seeds (for garnish)
- Sliced cucumber
- Cherry tomatoes
- Orange slices or other fresh fruit
- Soy sauce (for dipping)

Instructions:

Chicken Yakisoba:

Cook the soba or yakisoba noodles according to the package instructions. Drain and set aside.
In a large pan or wok, heat vegetable oil over medium-high heat.
Add sliced chicken and cook until browned and cooked through. Remove chicken from the pan and set aside.
In the same pan, add a bit more oil if needed. Sauté garlic until fragrant.

Add sliced onions, julienned carrots, and bell pepper. Cook until vegetables are slightly tender.

Add shredded cabbage and continue to cook until all vegetables are tender-crisp.

Return the cooked chicken to the pan.

In a small bowl, mix together soy sauce, oyster sauce, Worcestershire sauce, ketchup, sugar, salt, and pepper.

Pour the sauce over the chicken and vegetables, then add the cooked noodles. Toss everything together until well combined and heated through.

Taste and adjust the seasoning if necessary.

Garnish with chopped green onions.

Bento Box Assembly:

Place a portion of cooked rice in one section of the bento box.

Spoon a generous portion of Chicken Yakisoba next to the rice.

Arrange pickled ginger, sliced cucumber, and cherry tomatoes in separate sections.

Sprinkle sesame seeds over the Chicken Yakisoba for added flavor and texture.

Add slices of orange or other fresh fruit for a refreshing touch.

Include a small container of soy sauce for dipping.

Serving:

Enjoy your Chicken Yakisoba Bento by mixing the noodles and vegetables with the flavorful chicken. Dip each bite in soy sauce for an extra burst of umami. This bento provides a satisfying and balanced meal with a combination of protein, carbs, and vegetables.

Tuna Salad Onigirazu Bento

Ingredients:

For Tuna Salad Onigirazu:

- Cooked sushi rice
- Nori (seaweed) sheets
- Canned tuna, drained
- Mayonnaise
- Dijon mustard
- Salt and pepper to taste
- Avocado, sliced
- Lettuce leaves
- Thinly sliced cucumber
- Sliced tomatoes
- Optional: Pickled radishes or pickles for extra flavor

For Bento Box:

- Sushi rice (seasoned with rice vinegar, sugar, and salt)
- Pickled ginger
- Soy sauce for dipping
- Edamame (steamed and lightly salted)
- Sliced strawberries or other fresh fruits for dessert

Instructions:

Tuna Salad Onigirazu:

In a bowl, mix the canned tuna with mayonnaise, Dijon mustard, salt, and pepper. Adjust the quantities to your taste preferences.
Lay out a sheet of plastic wrap on a clean surface and place a nori sheet on top, shiny side down.
Take a handful of sushi rice and spread it evenly on the nori, leaving a border around the edges.
Place a layer of tuna salad on the rice, followed by avocado slices, lettuce leaves, cucumber, and sliced tomatoes. Add pickled radishes or pickles if desired.
Top with another layer of sushi rice.
Fold the edges of the nori sheet over the filling, creating a square or rectangular shape.

Wrap the onigirazu tightly in the plastic wrap and let it sit for a minute to help the nori stick together.

Repeat the process for additional onigirazu.

Bento Box Assembly:

Place a portion of seasoned sushi rice in one section of the bento box.

Unwrap the Tuna Salad Onigirazu and slice it into halves or quarters.

Arrange the onigirazu pieces in another section of the bento box.

Add pickled ginger and a small dipping sauce container for soy sauce.

Include a portion of steamed and lightly salted edamame in another compartment.

Complete the bento with a section of sliced strawberries or other fresh fruits for dessert.

Serving:

Enjoy your Tuna Salad Onigirazu Bento by dipping the onigirazu in soy sauce and savoring the combination of flavors and textures. It's a tasty and satisfying meal that's perfect for lunch.

Hijiki Seaweed Salad Bento

Ingredients:

- 1 cup dried hijiki seaweed
- 2 carrots, julienned
- 1/2 cup soy sauce
- 3 tablespoons rice vinegar
- 2 tablespoons sesame oil
- 1 tablespoon sugar
- 1 tablespoon mirin (optional)
- 1 tablespoon toasted sesame seeds
- 2 green onions, thinly sliced
- 1 teaspoon grated ginger

Instructions:

Rinse the dried hijiki seaweed thoroughly and soak it in water for about 15-20 minutes until it becomes tender.

In a pot, bring water to a boil and blanch the julienned carrots for about 2 minutes. Drain and set aside.

In a bowl, mix soy sauce, rice vinegar, sesame oil, sugar, and mirin to create the dressing.

Heat a pan and sauté the soaked hijiki seaweed for a few minutes. Add the carrots and continue cooking for another 2-3 minutes.

Pour the dressing over the hijiki and carrot mixture, tossing gently to combine.

Remove from heat and let it cool. Once cooled, sprinkle with sesame seeds, green onions, and grated ginger.

Bento Box Assembly:

Base Layer (Rice or Quinoa):
- Add a portion of cooked rice or quinoa to one section of the bento box.

Main Course (Hijiki Seaweed Salad):
- Place a generous portion of the hijiki seaweed salad in another section.

Protein (Choose one or a combination):
- Grilled chicken slices
- Teriyaki tofu cubes
- Edamame beans

Vegetable Side:
- Add a variety of sliced and colorful vegetables such as cherry tomatoes, cucumber sticks, or steamed broccoli in a section.

Fruit Section:

- Include fresh fruit like sliced strawberries, grapes, or orange segments for a sweet touch.

Garnish:
- Sprinkle some extra sesame seeds or chopped cilantro as a finishing touch.

Sauce or Dip:
- Include a small container with soy sauce or a dipping sauce of your choice.

Remember to pack utensils and enjoy your delicious and well-balanced Hijiki Seaweed Salad Bento!

Bulgogi Beef Bento

Ingredients:

- 1 pound thinly sliced beef (ribeye or sirloin)
- 1/2 cup soy sauce
- 3 tablespoons brown sugar
- 2 tablespoons mirin
- 1 tablespoon sesame oil
- 1 pear, grated
- 3 cloves garlic, minced
- 1 teaspoon grated ginger
- 2 tablespoons vegetable oil (for cooking)
- Sesame seeds and sliced green onions for garnish

Instructions:

In a bowl, mix soy sauce, brown sugar, mirin, sesame oil, grated pear, minced garlic, and grated ginger to create the marinade.
Add the thinly sliced beef to the marinade, ensuring each piece is coated.
Marinate for at least 30 minutes, or ideally, refrigerate for a few hours or overnight.
Heat vegetable oil in a pan over medium-high heat.
Cook the marinated beef in the pan until browned and cooked through, usually 2-3 minutes per side.
Garnish with sesame seeds and sliced green onions.

Bento Box Assembly:

Base Layer (Rice):
- Add a generous portion of steamed white or brown rice to one section of the bento box.

Main Course (Bulgogi Beef):
- Place a serving of the cooked Bulgogi Beef in another section.

Vegetable Side:
- Include stir-fried or steamed vegetables like broccoli, bell peppers, or carrots in a section.

Egg Roll or Tamagoyaki:
- Add a slice of egg roll or tamagoyaki (Japanese rolled omelet) for a protein boost.

Pickled Vegetables:

- Include some pickled cucumbers, radishes, or kimchi for a tangy and crunchy element.

Garnish:
- Garnish the Bulgogi Beef with additional sesame seeds and green onions.

Fruit Section:
- Add a serving of fresh fruit such as pineapple chunks or mandarin orange slices.

Sauce or Dip:
- Include a small container with extra Bulgogi marinade or a dipping sauce of your choice.

Remember to pack utensils and enjoy your flavorful Bulgogi Beef Bento!

Tamago Sushi Bento

Ingredients:

- 4 large eggs
- 2 tablespoons sugar
- 2 tablespoons mirin
- 2 tablespoons soy sauce
- 1 tablespoon vegetable oil

Instructions:

In a bowl, whisk together eggs, sugar, mirin, and soy sauce until well combined.
Heat a non-stick pan over medium-low heat and add vegetable oil.
Pour a thin layer of the egg mixture into the pan, tilting to spread it evenly. Cook until the edges start to set.
Roll the cooked egg from one side to the other using a spatula. Move the rolled egg to one side of the pan.
Add a bit more of the egg mixture to the empty side of the pan, lifting the rolled egg to let the new mixture flow underneath. Roll again.
Repeat the process until all the egg mixture is used and a thick, layered omelet is formed.
Once cooked, let the omelet cool and slice it into thin strips.

Bento Box Assembly:

Base Layer (Sushi Rice):
- Add a layer of seasoned sushi rice to one section of the bento box. You can mix the rice with a bit of rice vinegar, sugar, and salt for flavor.

Tamago Sushi Rolls:
- Place a sheet of nori on a bamboo sushi rolling mat.
- Spread a thin layer of sushi rice over the nori, leaving a small border at the top.
- Arrange slices of the Tamago omelet in the center.
- Roll the sushi tightly using the mat, sealing the edge with a bit of water.
- Slice the roll into bite-sized pieces.

Vegetable Side:
- Add a section with a mix of fresh vegetables like cucumber or avocado slices.

Edamame or Pickled Vegetables:

- Include edamame beans or pickled vegetables for a flavorful and nutritious side.

Garnish:
- Garnish the bento with sesame seeds, sliced green onions, or a sprinkle of furikake (Japanese seasoning).

Soy Sauce:
- Include a small container with soy sauce or tamari for dipping.

Fruit Section:
- Add a serving of fresh fruit such as grapes, berries, or melon.

Remember to pack chopsticks or a fork, and enjoy your delicious Tamago Sushi Bento!

Spinach and Mushroom Salad Bento

Ingredients:

- 4 cups fresh spinach leaves, washed and dried
- 1 cup sliced mushrooms (button or cremini)
- 1/4 cup red onion, thinly sliced
- 1/4 cup feta cheese, crumbled
- 1/4 cup walnuts, toasted
- 2 tablespoons balsamic vinegar
- 1 tablespoon olive oil
- Salt and pepper to taste

Instructions:

In a large bowl, combine fresh spinach, sliced mushrooms, red onion, crumbled feta cheese, and toasted walnuts.

In a small bowl, whisk together balsamic vinegar and olive oil. Season with salt and pepper to taste.

Drizzle the dressing over the salad and toss gently to coat all the ingredients.

Bento Box Assembly:

Base Layer (Quinoa or Couscous):
- Add a layer of cooked and cooled quinoa or couscous to one section of the bento box.

Spinach and Mushroom Salad:
- Place a generous portion of the prepared Spinach and Mushroom Salad in another section.

Protein (Grilled Chicken or Tofu):
- Include a serving of grilled chicken slices or tofu cubes for added protein.

Fresh Fruit Section:
- Add a section with fresh fruit such as apple slices, grapes, or berries.

Cheese and Crackers:
- Include a small compartment with a few whole-grain crackers and a serving of your favorite cheese.

Dressing or Hummus Dip:
- Pack a small container with extra balsamic dressing for drizzling over the salad or a side of hummus for dipping.

Garnish:

- Sprinkle some extra toasted walnuts or seeds on top of the salad for added crunch.

Water or Green Tea:
- Don't forget to include a small bottle of water or a container of green tea to stay hydrated.

Remember to pack utensils and enjoy your nutritious and flavorful Spinach and Mushroom Salad Bento!

Kani Salad Bento

Ingredients:

- 1 package (about 8 oz) imitation crab (kani), shredded
- 1 cucumber, julienned
- 1/2 cup mayonnaise
- 1 tablespoon sriracha sauce (adjust to taste)
- 1 teaspoon soy sauce
- 1 teaspoon rice vinegar
- 1 teaspoon sugar
- Sesame seeds for garnish

Instructions:

In a bowl, combine shredded imitation crab and julienned cucumber.
In a separate bowl, mix mayonnaise, sriracha sauce, soy sauce, rice vinegar, and sugar to create the dressing.
Pour the dressing over the crab and cucumber mixture, tossing gently to coat.
Chill the salad in the refrigerator for at least 30 minutes.
Sprinkle sesame seeds over the salad just before serving.

Bento Box Assembly:

Base Layer (Sushi Rice or Mixed Greens):
- Add a layer of seasoned sushi rice or a bed of mixed greens to one section of the bento box.

Kani Salad:
- Place a generous portion of the chilled Kani Salad in another section.

Edamame or Pickled Vegetables:
- Include edamame beans or pickled vegetables for added color and flavor.

Tamagoyaki (Japanese Rolled Omelet) or Egg Slices:
- Add a slice of tamagoyaki or some boiled and sliced eggs for protein.

Fresh Fruit Section:
- Include a section with fresh fruit such as pineapple chunks, orange slices, or strawberries.

Garnish:
- Garnish the Kani Salad with additional sesame seeds for an extra crunch.

Soy Sauce or Ginger Dressing:
- Pack a small container with soy sauce for dipping or a light ginger dressing for drizzling over the salad.

Chopsticks or Fork:
- Remember to pack chopsticks or a fork for easy eating.

Enjoy your delicious and satisfying Kani Salad Bento!

Nikujaga Bento

Ingredients:

- 1 pound thinly sliced beef
- 4 medium potatoes, peeled and cut into bite-sized pieces
- 2 carrots, peeled and sliced
- 1 onion, thinly sliced
- 1 cup green beans, trimmed and halved
- 1/4 cup soy sauce
- 3 tablespoons mirin
- 2 tablespoons sake (Japanese rice wine)
- 2 tablespoons sugar
- 2 cups dashi stock (or substitute with water)
- 2 tablespoons vegetable oil

Instructions:

In a large pot, heat vegetable oil and sauté the sliced beef until browned.
Add sliced onions and cook until they become translucent.
Add potatoes, carrots, and green beans to the pot.
In a bowl, mix soy sauce, mirin, sake, sugar, and dashi stock. Pour this mixture into the pot.
Bring the mixture to a boil, then reduce the heat to low and simmer until the vegetables are tender and the flavors meld together (usually around 20-30 minutes).

Bento Box Assembly:

Base Layer (Steamed Rice):
- Add a generous portion of steamed white or brown rice to one section of the bento box.

Nikujaga:
- Place a serving of the prepared Nikujaga in another section.

Tamagoyaki (Japanese Rolled Omelet) or Egg Slices:
- Add a slice of tamagoyaki or some boiled and sliced eggs for additional protein.

Pickled Vegetables:
- Include pickled vegetables, such as radishes or cucumbers, for a tangy contrast.

Seaweed Salad or Edamame:

- Add a section with seaweed salad or steamed edamame for a light and nutritious side.

Garnish:
- Garnish the Nikujaga with chopped green onions or a sprinkle of sesame seeds.

Soy Sauce or Ponzu:
- Pack a small container with soy sauce or ponzu for dipping or drizzling over the Nikujaga.

Chopsticks or Fork:
- Don't forget to pack utensils for convenient eating.

Enjoy your hearty and flavorful Nikujaga Bento!

Chicken Teriyaki Onigirazu Bento

Ingredients:

For Teriyaki Chicken:

- 1 pound boneless, skinless chicken thighs, sliced
- 1/4 cup soy sauce
- 2 tablespoons mirin
- 1 tablespoon sake (Japanese rice wine)
- 2 tablespoons sugar
- 1 tablespoon vegetable oil

For Onigirazu:

- 4 sheets nori (seaweed)
- 4 cups sushi rice, cooked and seasoned
- Teriyaki chicken slices
- 1 cucumber, julienned
- 4 slices of your favorite cheese
- Teriyaki sauce (for drizzling)
- Sesame seeds (for garnish)

Instructions:

Teriyaki Chicken:

In a bowl, mix soy sauce, mirin, sake, and sugar to create the teriyaki sauce.
Heat vegetable oil in a pan over medium heat. Add sliced chicken and cook until browned.
Pour the teriyaki sauce over the chicken and cook until the sauce thickens and coats the chicken.

Onigirazu Assembly:

Place a sheet of nori on a clean surface.
Spread a layer of sushi rice over the nori, leaving a small border on all sides.
Place a portion of teriyaki chicken on the rice, followed by cucumber slices and a slice of cheese.
Drizzle teriyaki sauce over the fillings and sprinkle with sesame seeds.

Fold the sides of the nori towards the center, covering the fillings.
Fold the top and bottom to form a square or rectangular shape.
Wrap the Onigirazu in plastic wrap and let it sit for a few minutes to seal.
Repeat for the remaining Onigirazu.

Bento Box Assembly:

   Base Layer (Vegetable or Seaweed Salad):
   - Add a layer of vegetable or seaweed salad to one section of the bento box.

   Chicken Teriyaki Onigirazu:
   - Place one or two Chicken Teriyaki Onigirazu in another section.

   Edamame or Pickled Vegetables:
   - Include edamame beans or pickled vegetables for added color and flavor.

   Fruit Section:
   - Add a section with fresh fruit such as orange slices, pineapple chunks, or grapes.

   Garnish:
   - Garnish the bento with additional sesame seeds or chopped green onions.

   Soy Sauce or Teriyaki Dipping Sauce:
   - Pack a small container with soy sauce or teriyaki dipping sauce for the Onigirazu.

   Chopsticks or Fork:
   - Remember to pack chopsticks or a fork for easy eating.

Enjoy your delicious and satisfying Chicken Teriyaki Onigirazu Bento!

Shrimp and Vegetable Tempura Bento

Ingredients:

For Tempura Batter:

- 1 cup all-purpose flour
- 1 cup ice-cold water
- 1 egg
- Ice cubes

For Shrimp and Vegetables:

- Shrimp, peeled and deveined
- Assorted vegetables (zucchini, sweet potato, bell pepper, broccoli, etc.)
- Vegetable oil for frying

Instructions:

In a bowl, combine flour, ice-cold water, and an egg. Mix until just combined. It's okay if there are lumps; do not overmix.
Add a few ice cubes to the batter to keep it cold.

For Shrimp:

3. Dip shrimp in the tempura batter and fry in hot oil until golden brown. Drain on paper towels.

For Vegetables:

4. Dip vegetable slices in the tempura batter and fry until golden and crispy. Drain excess oil on paper towels.

Bento Box Assembly:

Base Layer (Sushi Rice or Noodles):
- Add a layer of seasoned sushi rice or a bed of noodles to one section of the bento box.

Shrimp and Vegetable Tempura:
- Place a generous portion of shrimp and vegetable tempura in another section.

Pickled Ginger or Radish:
- Include pickled ginger or pickled radish for a palate cleanser.

Edamame or Steamed Vegetables:
- Add a section with edamame beans or lightly steamed vegetables.

Soy Dipping Sauce:
- Pack a small container with soy sauce or tempura dipping sauce for dipping the tempura.

Fresh Fruit Section:
- Include a section with fresh fruit such as orange slices, strawberries, or pineapple chunks.

Garnish:
- Garnish the bento with chopped green onions or sesame seeds.

Chopsticks or Fork:
- Remember to pack chopsticks or a fork for easy eating.

Ensure that the tempura is packed separately or placed strategically to maintain its crispiness until lunchtime. Enjoy your delicious Shrimp and Vegetable Tempura Bento!

Tofu and Wakame Salad Bento

Ingredients:

- 1/2 cup dried wakame seaweed
- 1 block firm tofu, pressed and cubed
- 1 cucumber, thinly sliced
- 1 carrot, julienned
- 1/4 cup soy sauce
- 2 tablespoons rice vinegar
- 1 tablespoon sesame oil
- 1 tablespoon mirin (optional)
- 1 tablespoon sugar
- 1 teaspoon grated ginger
- Sesame seeds for garnish
- Chopped green onions for garnish

Instructions:

Soak the dried wakame seaweed in warm water for about 10 minutes or until rehydrated. Drain and set aside.

In a bowl, combine the soy sauce, rice vinegar, sesame oil, mirin, sugar, and grated ginger to create the dressing.

In a large bowl, gently mix the rehydrated wakame, cubed tofu, cucumber slices, and julienned carrots.

Pour the dressing over the salad and toss gently to coat all the ingredients.

Let the salad marinate in the refrigerator for at least 30 minutes to allow the flavors to meld.

Garnish with sesame seeds and chopped green onions before serving.

Bento Box Assembly:

Base Layer (Brown Rice or Quinoa):
- Add a layer of cooked and cooled brown rice or quinoa to one section of the bento box.

Tofu and Wakame Salad:
- Place a generous portion of the Tofu and Wakame Salad in another section.

Edamame or Steamed Vegetables:
- Include edamame beans or a mix of lightly steamed vegetables for added color and nutrition.

Tamagoyaki (Japanese Rolled Omelet):

- Add a slice of tamagoyaki for a protein boost.

Fresh Fruit Section:
- Include a section with fresh fruit such as apple slices, grapes, or orange segments.

Garnish:
- Garnish the Tofu and Wakame Salad with additional sesame seeds and chopped green onions.

Soy Ginger Dressing:
- Pack a small container with extra soy ginger dressing or a light dipping sauce.

Chopsticks or Fork:
- Remember to pack chopsticks or a fork for easy eating.

Enjoy your nutritious and delicious Tofu and Wakame Salad Bento!

Pork and Kimchi Onigirazu Bento

Ingredients:

For Pork:

- 1/2 pound thinly sliced pork belly or pork shoulder
- 2 tablespoons soy sauce
- 1 tablespoon mirin
- 1 tablespoon sake
- 1 tablespoon sugar
- 1 teaspoon sesame oil
- 1 teaspoon grated ginger

For Onigirazu:

- 4 sheets nori (seaweed)
- 4 cups sushi rice, cooked and seasoned
- Cooked pork slices
- Kimchi, drained and chopped
- 4 slices of your favorite cheese
- Teriyaki sauce or gochujang (Korean red pepper paste)
- Sesame seeds for garnish

Instructions:

For Pork:

In a bowl, mix soy sauce, mirin, sake, sugar, sesame oil, and grated ginger.
Marinate the thinly sliced pork in the mixture for at least 30 minutes.
Cook the marinated pork in a pan until browned and cooked through.

For Onigirazu Assembly:

Place a sheet of nori on a clean surface.
Spread a layer of sushi rice over the nori, leaving a small border on all sides.
Place a slice of cheese in the center, followed by a portion of cooked pork and chopped kimchi.
Drizzle teriyaki sauce or gochujang over the fillings and sprinkle with sesame seeds.
Fold the sides of the nori towards the center, covering the fillings.

Fold the top and bottom to form a square or rectangular shape.
Wrap the Onigirazu in plastic wrap and let it sit for a few minutes to seal.
Repeat for the remaining Onigirazu.

Bento Box Assembly:

Base Layer (Vegetable or Seaweed Salad):
- Add a layer of vegetable or seaweed salad to one section of the bento box.

Pork and Kimchi Onigirazu:
- Place one or two Pork and Kimchi Onigirazu in another section.

Edamame or Steamed Vegetables:
- Include edamame beans or lightly steamed vegetables for added color and nutrition.

Fresh Fruit Section:
- Add a section with fresh fruit such as apple slices, pineapple chunks, or grapes.

Garnish:
- Garnish the bento with additional sesame seeds or chopped green onions.

Soy Sauce or Gochujang Dipping Sauce:
- Pack a small container with soy sauce or gochujang dipping sauce for the Onigirazu.

Chopsticks or Fork:
- Remember to pack chopsticks or a fork for easy eating.

Enjoy your delicious and flavorful Pork and Kimchi Onigirazu Bento!

Avocado and Cucumber Roll Bento

Ingredients:

- Nori sheets (seaweed)
- Sushi rice, seasoned with rice vinegar, sugar, and salt
- 1 ripe avocado, thinly sliced
- 1 cucumber, julienned
- Soy sauce, for dipping
- Pickled ginger, for serving
- Wasabi, for serving
- Sesame seeds, for garnish (optional)

Instructions:

Place a sheet of nori on a bamboo sushi rolling mat.
Wet your hands and spread a thin layer of sushi rice over the nori, leaving a small border at the top.
Arrange slices of avocado and julienned cucumber in the center of the rice.
Carefully roll the sushi using the bamboo mat, applying gentle pressure to shape it.
Seal the edge with a bit of water.
Repeat the process for additional rolls.
Using a sharp knife, slice each roll into bite-sized pieces.
Garnish with sesame seeds if desired.

Bento Box Assembly:

Base Layer (Sushi Rice or Quinoa):
- Add a layer of seasoned sushi rice or quinoa to one section of the bento box.

Avocado and Cucumber Rolls:
- Place a generous portion of the Avocado and Cucumber Rolls in another section.

Edamame or Steamed Vegetables:
- Include edamame beans or a mix of lightly steamed vegetables for added color and nutrition.

Tamagoyaki (Japanese Rolled Omelet) or Egg Slices:
- Add a slice of tamagoyaki or some boiled and sliced eggs for additional protein.

Pickled Vegetables:

- Include pickled vegetables, such as radishes or cucumbers, for a tangy contrast.

Garnish:
- Garnish the Avocado and Cucumber Rolls with sesame seeds or chopped green onions.

Soy Sauce, Pickled Ginger, and Wasabi:
- Pack small containers with soy sauce, pickled ginger, and a bit of wasabi for dipping.

Chopsticks or Fork:
- Remember to pack chopsticks or a fork for easy eating.

Enjoy your light and refreshing Avocado and Cucumber Roll Bento!

Beef Negimaki Bento

Ingredients:

- 1 pound thinly sliced beef (such as sirloin or flank steak)
- 4-5 green onions (scallions), cut into long strips
- 1/4 cup soy sauce
- 2 tablespoons mirin
- 2 tablespoons sake (Japanese rice wine)
- 1 tablespoon sugar
- 1 teaspoon grated ginger
- Bamboo skewers, soaked in water

Instructions:

In a bowl, mix soy sauce, mirin, sake, sugar, and grated ginger to create the marinade.
Marinate the beef slices in the mixture for at least 30 minutes.
Lay out a slice of beef, place a strip of green onion on top, and roll it up tightly.
Secure with a bamboo skewer.
Repeat the process for the remaining beef slices.
Grill the beef rolls on a hot grill or in a grill pan until the beef is cooked and slightly caramelized.

Bento Box Assembly:

Base Layer (Steamed Rice or Soba Noodles):
- Add a layer of steamed white or brown rice or cooked soba noodles to one section of the bento box.

Beef Negimaki Rolls:
- Place the Beef Negimaki Rolls in another section.

Vegetable Side:
- Include a mix of stir-fried or steamed vegetables such as broccoli, bell peppers, or snap peas.

Tamagoyaki (Japanese Rolled Omelet):
- Add a slice of tamagoyaki or some boiled and sliced eggs for additional protein.

Pickled Vegetables:
- Include pickled vegetables, such as radishes or cucumbers, for a tangy element.

Garnish:

- Garnish the bento with sesame seeds and chopped green onions.

Soy Dipping Sauce:
- Pack a small container with extra soy sauce or a dipping sauce of your choice for the Beef Negimaki.

Chopsticks or Fork:
- Remember to pack chopsticks or a fork for easy eating.

Enjoy your flavorful and satisfying Beef Negimaki Bento!

Chicken and Vegetable Skewers Bento

Ingredients:

For Chicken Marinade:

- 1 pound boneless, skinless chicken breasts or thighs, cut into cubes
- 2 tablespoons soy sauce
- 1 tablespoon olive oil
- 1 tablespoon honey
- 1 teaspoon garlic powder
- 1 teaspoon smoked paprika
- Salt and pepper to taste

For Vegetable Skewers:

- Bell peppers, cut into chunks
- Cherry tomatoes
- Red onion, cut into chunks
- Zucchini or yellow squash, sliced

For Skewers:

- Wooden or metal skewers (if using wooden skewers, soak them in water for 30 minutes before grilling)

Instructions:

In a bowl, mix together the soy sauce, olive oil, honey, garlic powder, smoked paprika, salt, and pepper to create the marinade.

Marinate the chicken cubes in the mixture for at least 30 minutes.

Thread the marinated chicken and vegetables onto the skewers, alternating between chicken and veggies.

Grill the skewers on a barbecue or grill pan until the chicken is cooked through and the vegetables are charred.

Bento Box Assembly:

Base Layer (Quinoa or Brown Rice):
- Add a layer of cooked and cooled quinoa or brown rice to one section of the bento box.

Chicken and Vegetable Skewers:
- Place the grilled Chicken and Vegetable Skewers in another section.

Fresh Fruit Section:
- Include a section with fresh fruit such as pineapple chunks, grapes, or apple slices.

Greek Salad:
- Add a small compartment with a simple Greek salad, including cucumber, cherry tomatoes, feta cheese, and olives.

Garnish:
- Garnish the bento with a sprinkle of fresh herbs like parsley or mint.

Tzatziki Sauce or Hummus:
- Pack a small container with tzatziki sauce or hummus for dipping the skewers or enjoying with the salad.

Chopsticks or Fork:
- Remember to pack chopsticks or a fork for easy eating.

Enjoy your delicious and well-balanced Chicken and Vegetable Skewers Bento!

Quinoa and Avocado Salad Bento

Ingredients:

- 1 cup quinoa, rinsed
- 2 cups water
- 1 large avocado, diced
- 1 cup cherry tomatoes, halved
- 1/2 cucumber, diced
- 1/4 cup red onion, finely chopped
- 1/4 cup fresh cilantro or parsley, chopped
- Juice of 1 lime
- 2 tablespoons olive oil
- Salt and pepper to taste

Instructions:

In a saucepan, combine quinoa and water. Bring to a boil, then reduce heat to low, cover, and simmer for 15-20 minutes or until quinoa is cooked and water is absorbed.
Fluff the quinoa with a fork and let it cool to room temperature.
In a large bowl, combine the cooked quinoa, diced avocado, cherry tomatoes, cucumber, red onion, and cilantro.
In a small bowl, whisk together lime juice, olive oil, salt, and pepper.
Pour the dressing over the quinoa mixture and toss gently to combine.
Adjust seasoning if necessary and refrigerate for at least 30 minutes before serving.

Bento Box Assembly:

Base Layer (Quinoa Salad):
- Add a generous portion of the Quinoa and Avocado Salad to one section of the bento box.

Protein (Grilled Chicken or Chickpeas):
- Include a serving of grilled chicken slices or roasted chickpeas for added protein.

Fresh Vegetable Sticks:
- Add a section with colorful vegetable sticks such as bell peppers, carrots, or celery for a crunchy element.

Cheese and Crackers:

- Include a small compartment with a few whole-grain crackers and a serving of your favorite cheese.

Fresh Fruit Section:
- Add a section with fresh fruit such as apple slices, grapes, or berries.

Garnish:
- Garnish the Quinoa and Avocado Salad with additional cilantro or a sprinkle of seeds like sunflower or pumpkin seeds.

Lime Wedge:
- Pack a small lime wedge for an extra burst of citrus flavor.

Dressing or Hummus Dip:
- Include a small container with extra lime vinaigrette or a side of hummus for dipping.

Remember to pack utensils and enjoy your nutritious and delicious Quinoa and Avocado Salad Bento!

Sesame Chicken Bento

Ingredients:

For Chicken:

- 1 pound boneless, skinless chicken breasts or thighs, cut into bite-sized pieces
- 1/4 cup soy sauce
- 2 tablespoons honey
- 1 tablespoon sesame oil
- 2 cloves garlic, minced
- 1 teaspoon grated ginger
- 1 tablespoon cornstarch
- Sesame seeds for garnish

For Sauce:

- 2 tablespoons soy sauce
- 1 tablespoon rice vinegar
- 1 tablespoon hoisin sauce
- 1 tablespoon honey

Instructions:

In a bowl, combine soy sauce, honey, sesame oil, minced garlic, grated ginger, and cornstarch to make the marinade.
Marinate the chicken pieces in the mixture for at least 30 minutes.
In a pan or wok, cook the marinated chicken over medium-high heat until fully cooked and browned.
In a small saucepan, mix together the ingredients for the sauce and heat until well combined and slightly thickened.
Pour the sauce over the cooked chicken, toss to coat, and let it simmer for an additional 2-3 minutes.
Garnish with sesame seeds before serving.

Bento Box Assembly:

Base Layer (Steamed Rice or Noodles):
- Add a layer of steamed white or brown rice or cooked noodles to one section of the bento box.

Sesame Chicken:

- Place a generous portion of the Sesame Chicken in another section.

Vegetable Stir-Fry:
- Include a mix of colorful stir-fried vegetables such as broccoli, bell peppers, and snap peas.

Pickled Cucumbers or Radishes:
- Add a section with lightly pickled cucumbers or radishes for a refreshing touch.

Fresh Fruit Section:
- Include a section with fresh fruit such as orange slices, pineapple chunks, or apple slices.

Garnish:
- Garnish the Sesame Chicken with additional sesame seeds and chopped green onions.

Soy Sauce or Teriyaki Dipping Sauce:
- Pack a small container with soy sauce or teriyaki dipping sauce for extra flavor.

Chopsticks or Fork:
- Remember to pack chopsticks or a fork for easy eating.

Enjoy your delicious and flavorful Sesame Chicken Bento!

Chirashi Sushi Bento

Ingredients:

For Sushi Rice:

- 2 cups sushi rice, washed and cooked
- 1/3 cup rice vinegar
- 3 tablespoons sugar
- 1 teaspoon salt

For Toppings:

- Sashimi-grade fish (salmon, tuna, shrimp, etc.), thinly sliced
- Cooked and seasoned crab or imitation crab
- Tamagoyaki (Japanese rolled omelet), sliced
- Avocado, sliced
- Cucumber, julienned
- Pickled ginger
- Sesame seeds for garnish
- Soy sauce and wasabi for serving

Instructions:

Mix rice vinegar, sugar, and salt in a bowl. Heat in the microwave for 30 seconds, stirring until sugar and salt dissolve.
While the rice is still warm, gently fold in the vinegar mixture to season the rice.
Let it cool to room temperature.
Spread the seasoned sushi rice in the bento box.

Assembling Chirashi Sushi Bento:

Base Layer (Sushi Rice):
- Add a layer of seasoned sushi rice to the bottom of the bento box.

Assorted Toppings:
- Arrange a variety of toppings over the rice, including slices of sashimi-grade fish, crab, tamagoyaki, avocado, cucumber, and pickled ginger.

Garnish:
- Sprinkle sesame seeds over the toppings for added texture and flavor.

Soy Sauce and Wasabi:

- Pack small containers with soy sauce and wasabi for dipping.

Edamame or Seaweed Salad:
- Include a side section with edamame beans or a small serving of seaweed salad.

Fresh Fruit Section:
- Add a section with fresh fruit such as orange slices, pineapple chunks, or berries.

Chopsticks or Fork:
- Remember to pack chopsticks or a fork for easy eating.

Chirashi Sushi allows for creativity, so feel free to customize the toppings based on your preferences. Enjoy your beautiful and delicious Chirashi Sushi Bento!

Egg Salad Onigirazu Bento

Ingredients:

For Egg Salad:

- 6 hard-boiled eggs, chopped
- 1/4 cup mayonnaise
- 1 tablespoon Dijon mustard
- Salt and pepper to taste
- Chopped chives or green onions for garnish

For Onigirazu:

- 2 sheets nori (seaweed)
- 2 cups sushi rice, cooked and seasoned
- Egg salad mixture
- Lettuce leaves
- Sliced tomatoes
- Optional: Avocado slices, pickles, or other favorite fillings
- Soy sauce or your favorite dipping sauce

Instructions:

For Egg Salad:

In a bowl, combine chopped hard-boiled eggs, mayonnaise, Dijon mustard, salt, and pepper. Mix well.
Fold in chopped chives or green onions for added flavor.

For Onigirazu Assembly:

Place a sheet of nori on a clean surface.
Spread a layer of sushi rice over the nori, leaving a small border on all sides.
Spread a generous portion of the egg salad over the rice.
Add lettuce leaves, sliced tomatoes, and any optional fillings.
Fold the sides of the nori towards the center, covering the fillings.
Fold the top and bottom to form a square or rectangular shape.
Wrap the Egg Salad Onigirazu in plastic wrap and let it sit for a few minutes to seal.
Repeat for the second Onigirazu.

Bento Box Assembly:

- Base Layer (Vegetable or Seaweed Salad):
  - Add a layer of vegetable or seaweed salad to one section of the bento box.
- Egg Salad Onigirazu:
  - Place one or two Egg Salad Onigirazu in another section.
- Edamame or Pickled Vegetables:
  - Include edamame beans or pickled vegetables for added color and flavor.
- Fresh Fruit Section:
  - Add a section with fresh fruit such as apple slices, grapes, or melon cubes.
- Garnish:
  - Garnish the bento with additional chives or green onions for a pop of color.
- Soy Sauce or Dipping Sauce:
  - Pack a small container with soy sauce or your favorite dipping sauce for the Onigirazu.
- Chopsticks or Fork:
  - Remember to pack chopsticks or a fork for easy eating.

Enjoy your delicious and portable Egg Salad Onigirazu Bento!

Green Bean and Sesame Salad Bento

Ingredients:

- 2 cups green beans, trimmed and blanched
- 1 tablespoon sesame oil
- 1 tablespoon soy sauce
- 1 tablespoon rice vinegar
- 1 teaspoon sugar
- 1 teaspoon grated ginger
- 1 clove garlic, minced
- 1 tablespoon sesame seeds, toasted
- Salt and pepper to taste

Instructions:

Blanch the green beans in boiling water for 2-3 minutes until they are bright green and still crisp. Transfer them to an ice bath to stop the cooking process. Drain and pat dry.
In a bowl, whisk together sesame oil, soy sauce, rice vinegar, sugar, grated ginger, minced garlic, salt, and pepper to make the dressing.
Toss the blanched green beans in the dressing until well coated.
Sprinkle toasted sesame seeds over the salad before serving.

Bento Box Assembly:

Base Layer (Quinoa or Brown Rice):
- Add a layer of cooked and cooled quinoa or brown rice to one section of the bento box.

Green Bean and Sesame Salad:
- Place a generous portion of the Green Bean and Sesame Salad in another section.

Protein (Grilled Chicken or Tofu):
- Include a serving of grilled chicken slices or tofu cubes for added protein.

Sliced Avocado:
- Add a section with slices of ripe avocado for a creamy texture.

Fresh Fruit Section:
- Include a section with fresh fruit such as orange slices, strawberries, or grapes.

Garnish:
- Garnish the bento with additional sesame seeds and chopped green onions.

Soy Ginger Dressing:
- Pack a small container with extra soy ginger dressing for drizzling over the salad.

Chopsticks or Fork:
- Remember to pack chopsticks or a fork for easy eating.

Enjoy your light and nutritious Green Bean and Sesame Salad Bento!

Shrimp and Avocado Onigiri Bento

Ingredients:

For Onigiri Rice:

- 2 cups sushi rice, washed and cooked
- 1/3 cup rice vinegar
- 3 tablespoons sugar
- 1 teaspoon salt

For Shrimp and Avocado Filling:

- Cooked shrimp, peeled and deveined
- Ripe avocado, sliced
- Soy sauce for brushing the shrimp
- Nori sheets, cut into strips for wrapping

For Onigiri Assembly:

- Sesame seeds for garnish
- Soy sauce or tamari for dipping

Instructions:

For Onigiri Rice:

Mix rice vinegar, sugar, and salt in a bowl. Heat in the microwave for 30 seconds, stirring until sugar and salt dissolve.
While the rice is still warm, gently fold in the vinegar mixture to season the rice.
Let it cool to room temperature.

For Shrimp and Avocado Filling:

Brush cooked shrimp with soy sauce and grill or sauté until fully cooked.
Cut avocado into slices.

For Onigiri Assembly:

Wet your hands and place a small amount of seasoned rice in the palm of your hand.

Place a slice of avocado and a grilled shrimp in the center.
Cover the filling with more rice and shape it into a triangular or round onigiri.
Wrap a strip of nori around the onigiri, securing it in place.
Repeat the process for the desired number of onigiri.
Sprinkle sesame seeds over the onigiri for garnish.

Bento Box Assembly:

Base Layer (Vegetable or Seaweed Salad):
- Add a layer of vegetable or seaweed salad to one section of the bento box.

Shrimp and Avocado Onigiri:
- Place one or two Shrimp and Avocado Onigiri in another section.

Edamame or Pickled Vegetables:
- Include edamame beans or pickled vegetables for added color and flavor.

Fresh Fruit Section:
- Add a section with fresh fruit such as mango slices, pineapple chunks, or kiwi.

Garnish:
- Garnish the bento with additional sesame seeds and sliced green onions.

Soy Sauce or Tamari:
- Pack a small container with soy sauce or tamari for dipping the onigiri.

Chopsticks or Fork:
- Remember to pack chopsticks or a fork for easy eating.

Enjoy your delicious and beautifully crafted Shrimp and Avocado Onigiri Bento!

Teriyaki Tofu and Broccoli Bento

Ingredients:

For Teriyaki Sauce:

- 1/4 cup soy sauce
- 2 tablespoons mirin
- 1 tablespoon sake (optional)
- 1 tablespoon sugar
- 1 teaspoon grated ginger
- 1 clove garlic, minced

For Tofu and Broccoli:

- 1 block firm tofu, pressed and cubed
- 2 cups broccoli florets
- 2 tablespoons vegetable oil
- Sesame seeds for garnish
- Green onions, chopped for garnish

Instructions:

For Teriyaki Sauce:

In a small saucepan, combine soy sauce, mirin, sake, sugar, grated ginger, and minced garlic.
Heat over medium heat, stirring until the sugar dissolves. Simmer for a few minutes until the sauce thickens slightly. Set aside.

For Tofu and Broccoli:

In a large skillet or wok, heat vegetable oil over medium-high heat.
Add cubed tofu and cook until golden brown on all sides.
Add broccoli florets to the skillet and stir-fry until they are tender-crisp.
Pour the teriyaki sauce over the tofu and broccoli, tossing to coat evenly.
Let it simmer for a few minutes until the sauce thickens and coats the tofu and broccoli.
Garnish with sesame seeds and chopped green onions.

Bento Box Assembly:

Base Layer (Brown Rice or Quinoa):
- Add a layer of cooked and cooled brown rice or quinoa to one section of the bento box.

Teriyaki Tofu and Broccoli:
- Place a generous portion of Teriyaki Tofu and Broccoli in another section.

Edamame or Steamed Vegetables:
- Include edamame beans or a mix of lightly steamed vegetables for added color and nutrition.

Fresh Fruit Section:
- Add a section with fresh fruit such as orange slices, grapes, or apple slices.

Garnish:
- Garnish the Teriyaki Tofu and Broccoli with additional sesame seeds and chopped green onions.

Soy Sauce Dipping Cup:
- Pack a small container with extra teriyaki sauce or soy sauce for dipping.

Chopsticks or Fork:
- Remember to pack chopsticks or a fork for easy eating.

Enjoy your delicious and wholesome Teriyaki Tofu and Broccoli Bento!

Soba Noodle Salad Bento

Ingredients:

For Soba Noodles:

- 8 ounces soba noodles
- 1 tablespoon sesame oil (for tossing noodles)

For Salad:

- 1 cup shredded cabbage
- 1 cup julienned carrots
- 1 cucumber, thinly sliced
- 1/2 cup edamame, cooked and shelled
- 2 green onions, sliced
- Sesame seeds for garnish

For Dressing:

- 3 tablespoons soy sauce
- 2 tablespoons rice vinegar
- 1 tablespoon sesame oil
- 1 tablespoon honey
- 1 teaspoon grated ginger
- 1 clove garlic, minced
- Red pepper flakes (optional for heat)

Instructions:

Cook soba noodles according to package instructions. Drain and toss with 1 tablespoon of sesame oil to prevent sticking. Let them cool to room temperature.
In a large bowl, combine shredded cabbage, julienned carrots, sliced cucumber, edamame, and green onions.
In a small bowl, whisk together soy sauce, rice vinegar, sesame oil, honey, grated ginger, minced garlic, and red pepper flakes if using.
Pour the dressing over the salad ingredients and toss to combine.
Add the cooled soba noodles to the salad and toss again until everything is well coated.
Garnish with sesame seeds before serving.

Bento Box Assembly:

- Base Layer (Soba Noodle Salad):
  - Add a generous portion of the Soba Noodle Salad to one section of the bento box.
- Protein (Grilled Chicken or Tofu):
  - Include a serving of grilled chicken slices or tofu cubes for added protein.
- Fresh Vegetable Sticks:
  - Add a section with colorful vegetable sticks such as bell peppers, carrots, or celery for a crunchy element.
- Seaweed Snacks or Nori Strips:
  - Include small portions of seaweed snacks or nori strips for a savory touch.
- Fresh Fruit Section:
  - Add a section with fresh fruit such as mandarin orange segments, berries, or sliced melon.
- Garnish:
  - Garnish the Soba Noodle Salad with additional sesame seeds and chopped cilantro or mint.
- Soy Sauce or Extra Dressing:
  - Pack a small container with soy sauce or extra dressing for drizzling over the noodles.
- Chopsticks or Fork:
  - Remember to pack chopsticks or a fork for easy eating.

Enjoy your delicious and cooling Soba Noodle Salad Bento!